# 100 Write-and-Learn
# Sight Word
## Practice Pages - Teaching Resources

**FREE !! Resoures Inside !!**

Engaging Reproducible Activity Pages That Help Kids

Recognize, Write, and Really LEARN the Top 100 High-Frequency

Words That are Key to Reading Success

## GRADES K-2

# This Book
## Belongs To:

_____

EMAIL US AT

scholasticzone@gmail.com

TO GET FREE GOODIES!

Just title the email "FREE Worksheets"

And we'll send you some extra worksheets for your kiddo!!

# Sight Word - I

Color it!

I

Name_____

Trace it!

Write it!

Cut and paste it!

_____ have an apple.

Find and color it!

she    on    I    he

I    in    I    the    I

I

# Sight Word - can

Name_____

**Color it!**

can

**Trace it!**

can can

**Write it!**

☐ ☐ ☐

**Connect the letters!**

c d n e g

k a f v o

I _____ swim.

**Find and color it!**

can on we at can

am can a it can

# Sight Word - we

Name_____

**Color it!**

we

**Trace it!**

we  we

**Write it!**

☐ ☐

**Connect the letters!**

a  e  r  n  k
w  b  b  p  i

_____ are friends.

**Find and color it!**

be  we  on  in  a
we  I  we  we  it

# Sight Word - the

Name_____

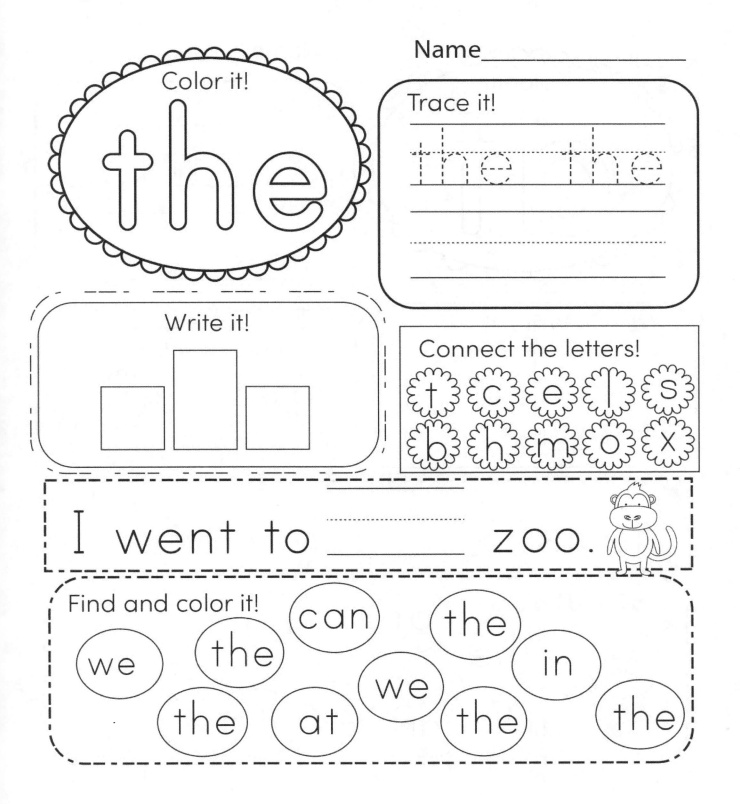

Color it!

**the**

Trace it!

the the

Write it!

Connect the letters!

t  c  e  l  s
b  h  m  o  x

I went to _____ zoo.

Find and color it!

we   the   can   the
the   at   we   the   in   the

# Sight Word - at

Name_____

**Color it!**

at

**Trace it!**

at at at

**Write it!**

**Connect the letters!**

a t f r n
v n p d h

He is _____ school.

**Find and color it!**

at · the · at · be · a
· at · at
at · can · in

# Sight Word – am

Name_____

**Color it!**

am

**Trace it!**

am      am

**Write it!**

**Connect the letters!**

v  m  s  d  n
a  g  c  e  k

I _____ sleepy.

**Find and color it!**

in    am    on    am
      be    am    at    are    am    am

# Sight Word - it

Name_____

Color it!

**it**

Trace it!

Write it!

Connect the letters!

i  n  w  o  x

e  t  a  p  z

_____ is a sunny day.

Find and color it!

at    it    can    it

it    I    it    be    I

# Sight Word - up

Name_____

Color it!

up

Trace it!

up    up

Write it!

Connect the letters!

a  p  k  x  y
u  e  g  q  s

I cleaned_____ my room.

Find and color it!

up    in    up    up    it
at    up    we    up
am

# Sight Word - no

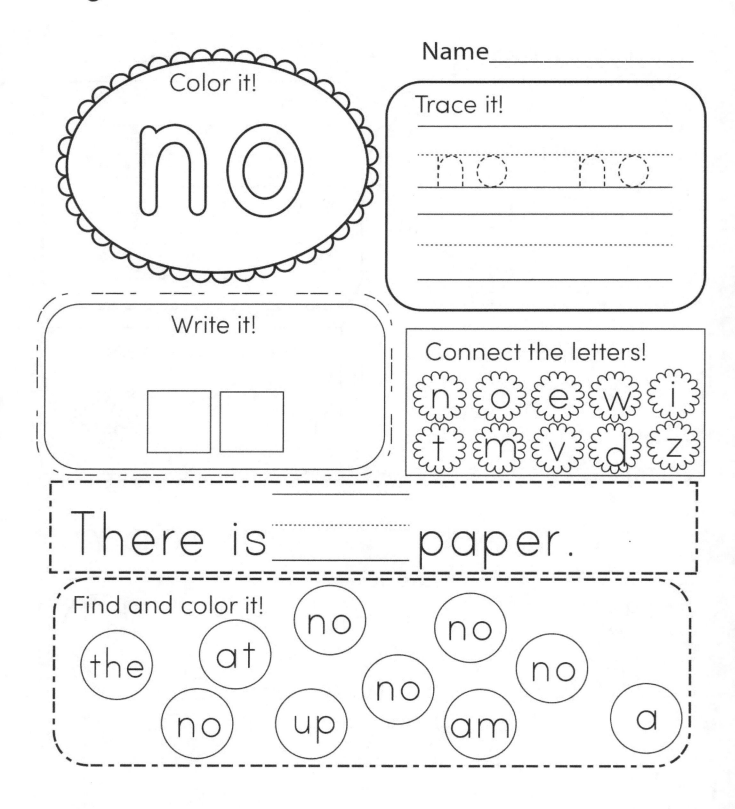

Name_____

**Color it!**

no

**Trace it!**

no   no

**Write it!**

☐ ☐

**Connect the letters!**

n  o  e  w  i
t  m  v  d  z

There is_____paper.

**Find and color it!**

the   at   no   no

no   up   no   am   no   a

# Sight Word - yes

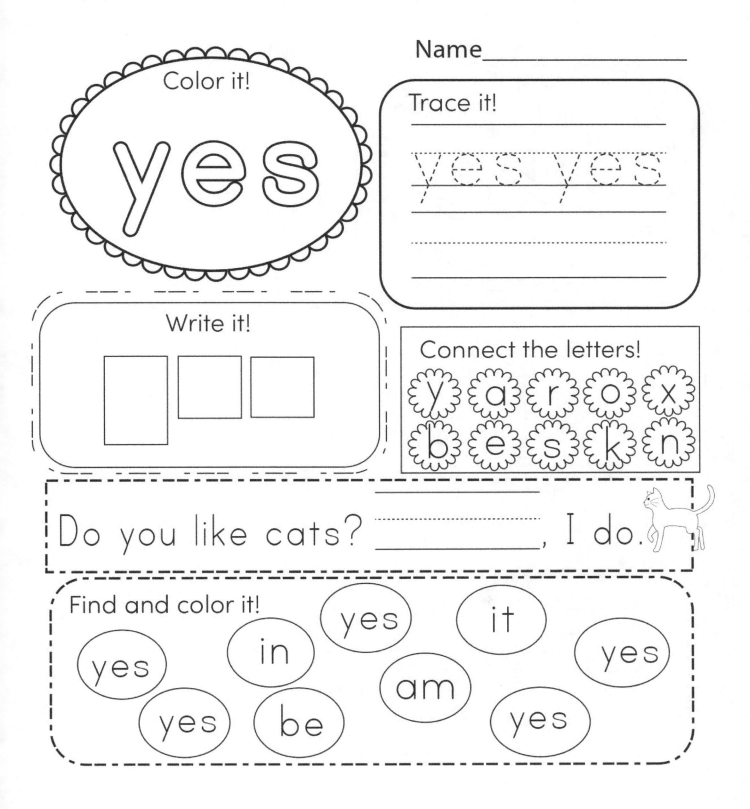

Name_____

**Color it!**

yes

**Trace it!**

yes yes

**Write it!**

**Connect the letters!**

y a r o x
b e s k n

Do you like cats? _____, I do.

**Find and color it!**

yes in yes it yes
yes be am yes

# Sight Word - like

Name_____

## Color it!

like

## Trace it!

like like

## Write it!

## Connect the letters!

n  e  k  e  h
l  i  o  t  w

I _____ lions.

## Find and color it!

yes    be    like    yes    like

like    can    like    like

# Sight Word - a

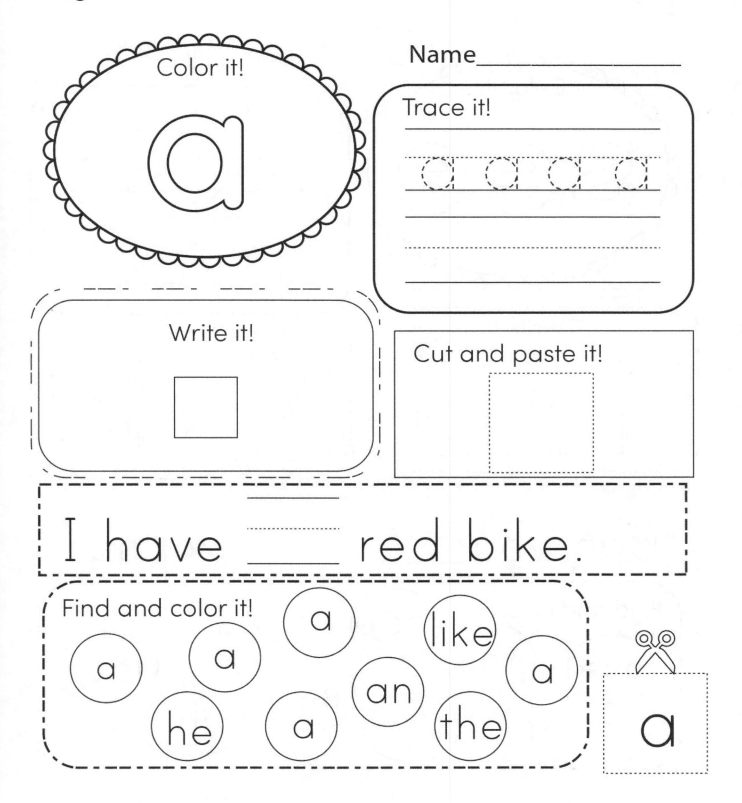

Color it!

a

Name_____

Trace it!

a   a   a   a

Write it!

Cut and paste it!

I have ____ red bike.

Find and color it!

a   a   a   like   a   he   an   the   a

a

# Sight Word - see

Name_____

**Color it!**

see

**Trace it!**

see see

**Write it!**

**Connect the letters!**

s e w u n
o v e t i

Can you_____ the house?

**Find and color it!**

see    the    see    see    look

at    see    see    in

# Sight Word - go

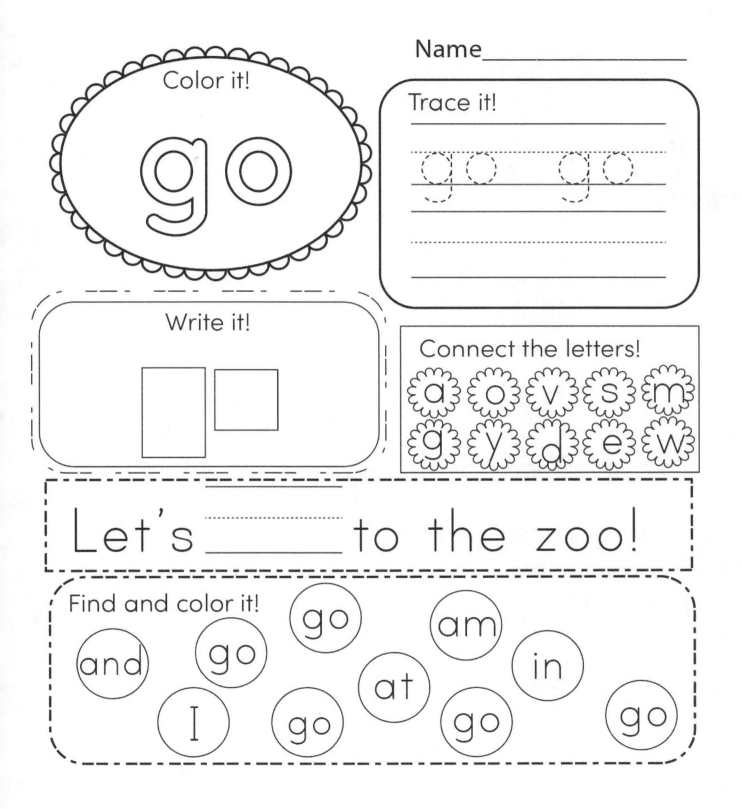

Color it!

**go**

Name_____

Trace it!

*go    go*

Write it!

Connect the letters!

a  o  v  s  m
g  y  d  e  w

Let's _____ to the zoo!

Find and color it!

and    go    go    am

I    go    at    go    in    go

# Sight Word - in

Name_____

**Color it!**

in

**Trace it!**

in   in   in

**Write it!**

**Connect the letters!**

i   n   b   n   a

c   e   s   m   z

I have a pen_____my bag.

**Find and color it!**

in   it   in   in   in

in   no   in   be   up

# Sight Word - of

**Color it!**

of

Name_____

**Trace it!**

o f    o f    o f

**Write it!**

**Connect the letters!**

a f n p a
o c w h s

She has a lot _____ friends.

**Find and color it!**

of  on  of  of  at
up  of  in  of  of

# Sight Word - us

Name_____

**Color it!**

**Trace it!**

us      us

**Write it!**

**Connect the letters!**

n  s  d  w  a
u  v  k  c  s

Rachel gave_____cookies.

**Find and color it!**

us   in   us   us   us
   us   up   us   on   is

# Sight Word - by

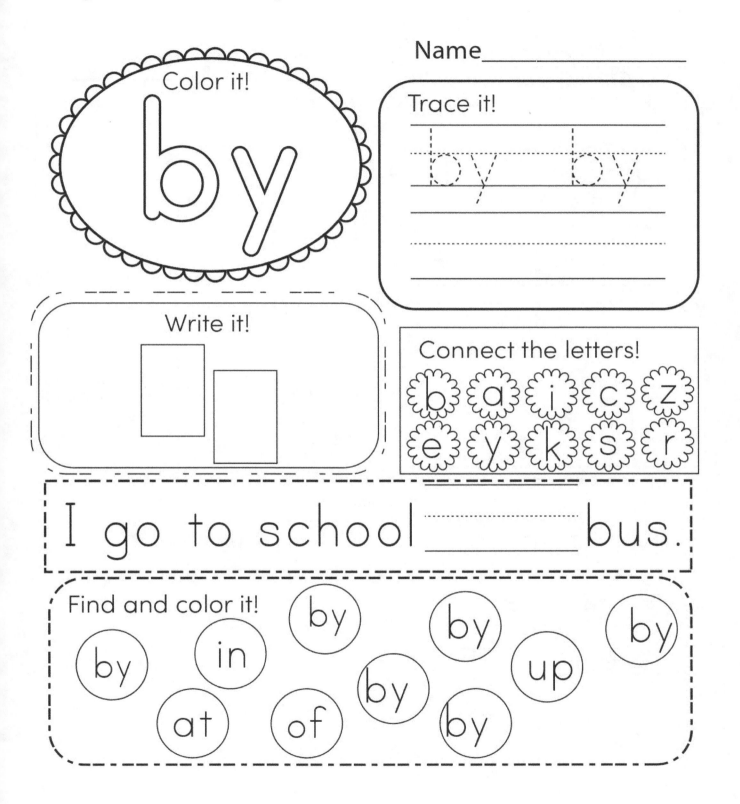

Color it!

**by**

Name_____

Trace it!

by    by

Write it!

Connect the letters!

b  a  i  c  z
e  y  k  s  r

I go to school _____ bus.

Find and color it!

by    in    by    by    by

at    of    by    up

by

# Sight Word - eat

Name_____

**Color it!**

eat

**Trace it!**

eat eat

**Write it!**

**Connect the letters!**

e a c x s
w e t k n

I want to _____ cookies.

**Find and color it!**

eat   in   yes   eat

like   eat   eat   eat   by

# Sight Word - was

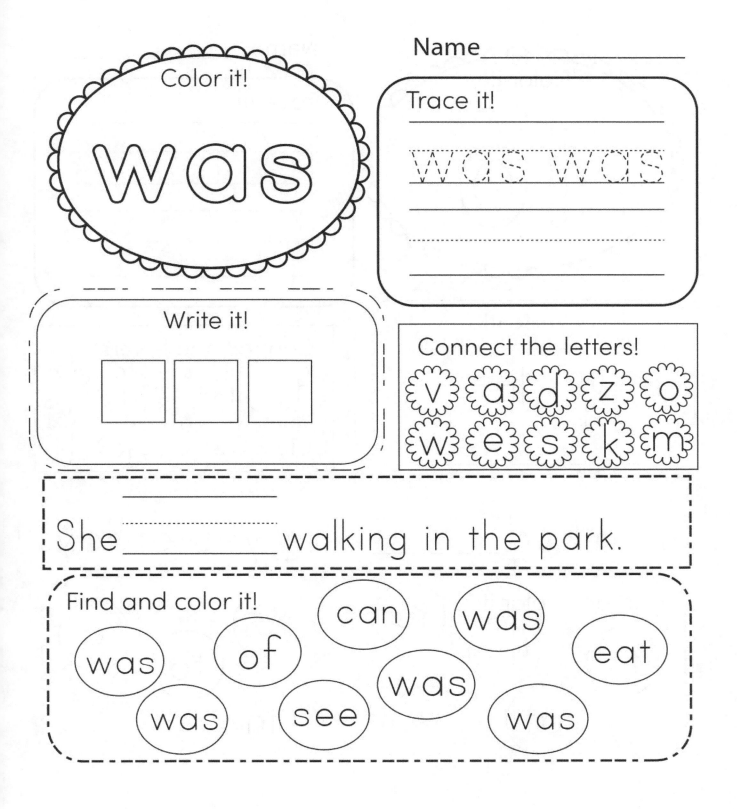

**Color it!**

was

**Name**_____

**Trace it!**

was was

**Write it!**

**Connect the letters!**

v a d z o
w e s k m

She_____ walking in the park.

**Find and color it!**

can   was
was   of         eat
was   see   was   was

# Sight Word - to

Name_____

**Color it!**

to

**Trace it!**

to   to   to

**Write it!**

**Connect the letters!**

t  u  x  r  n
a  o  c  k  h

I talked _____ Jim yesterday.

**Find and color it!**

to    the    to    to    a
at    to    by    to    in

# Sight Word - have

**Color it!**

have

Name_____

**Trace it!**

have

**Write it!**

**Connect the letters!**

n a k e c
h i v t x

I _____ a pet turtle.

**Find and color it!**

have   be   and   have   have   like   have   have   eat

# Sight Word - is

Name_____

### Color it!
is

### Trace it!
is   is   is

### Write it!

### Connect the letters!
i  u  x  g  n
a  s  c  p  h

My aunt _____ a teacher.

### Find and color it!
of   is   on   is   is
at   of   is   to
         is

# Sight Word – play

Name_____

**Color it!**

play

**Trace it!**

play

**Write it!**

**Connect the letters!**

n e a y h
p l o t x

I can _____ the piano.

**Find and color it!**

yes    play    play    play    play

of    can    play    like

# Sight Word - come

**Color it!**

come

Name_____

**Trace it!**

come

**Write it!**

☐ ☐ ☐ ☐

**Connect the letters!**

c  o  a  y  i
p  l  m  e  x

Will you _____ to the party?

**Find and color it!**

yes    play    come    come    come

come    can    come    like

# Sight Word - on

**Color it!**

on

Name_____

**Trace it!**

on      on

**Write it!**

☐ ☐

**Connect the letters!**

o  s  d  w  a
u  n  k  c  g

I read a book_____ Tuesday.

**Find and color it!**

on   on   of   on   in
us   on   by   is   on

# Sight Word - be

Name_____

**Color it!**

b e

**Trace it!**

be    be

**Write it!**

**Connect the letters!**

t e x r n
b o c k h

Will you _____ there?

**Find and color it!**

be   the   of   to   be

at   be   be   in

# Sight Word - big

Name_____

### Color it!
big

### Trace it!
big  big

### Write it!

### Connect the letters!
y i g e x
b o s k n

Elephants are _____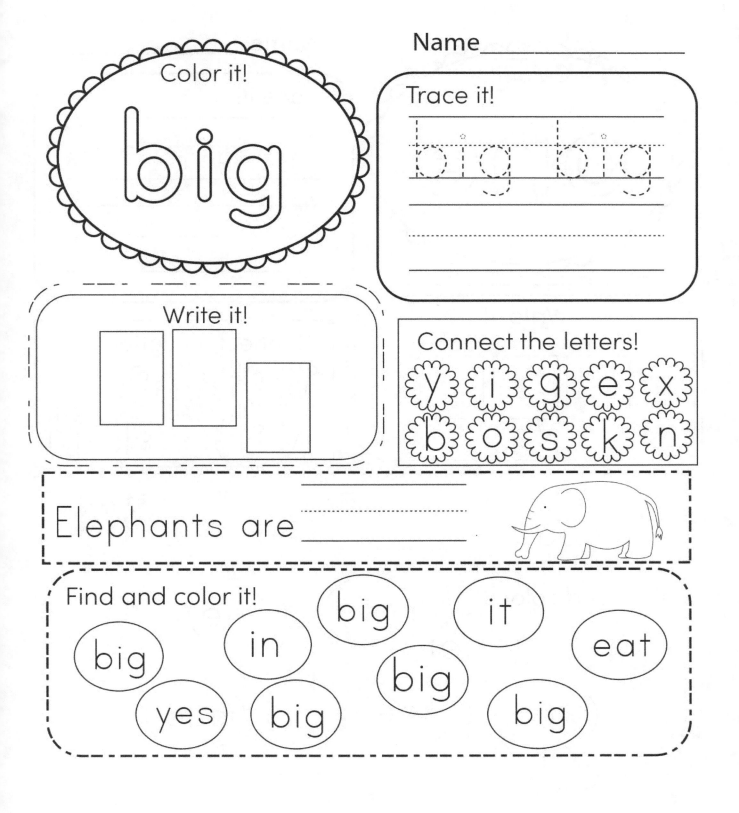

### Find and color it!
big    in    big    it    eat
yes    big    big    big

# Sight Word - one

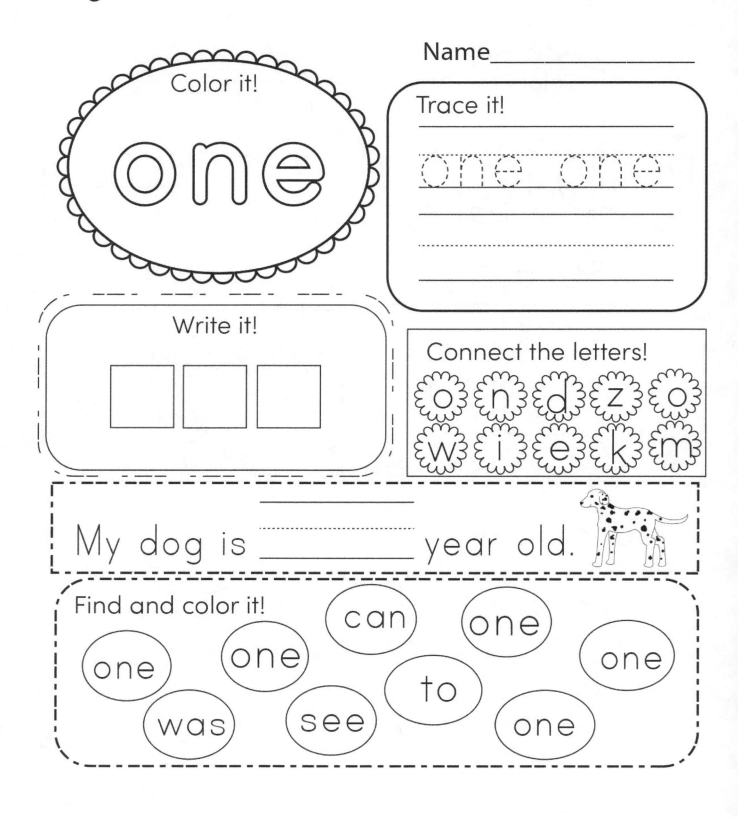

Color it!

one

Name_____

Trace it!

one one

Write it!

Connect the letters!

o n d z o
w l e k m

My dog is _____ year old.

Find and color it!

can    one
one         one
one
was    see    to    one

# Sight Word - has

Name_____

### Color it!
has

### Trace it!
has has

### Write it!

### Connect the letters!
h a r o x
b e s k n

She_____ a cute room.

### Find and color it!
has   has   can   has   yes
go   has   am   has

# Sight Word - are

Name_____

## Color it!

are

## Trace it!

are   are

## Write it!

☐ ☐ ☐

## Connect the letters!

o  r  d  z  o

a  i  e  k  m

The oranges _____ sweet.

## Find and color it!

can   are

are   are   one

are   to

was   are   are

# Sight Word - for

**Color it!**

for

**Name**_____

**Trace it!**

for for

**Write it!**

**Connect the letters!**

h a r o x
f o s k n

I got this gift _____ my sister.

**Find and color it!**

for    on    can    for    yes
for    has    for    for

# Sight Word - you

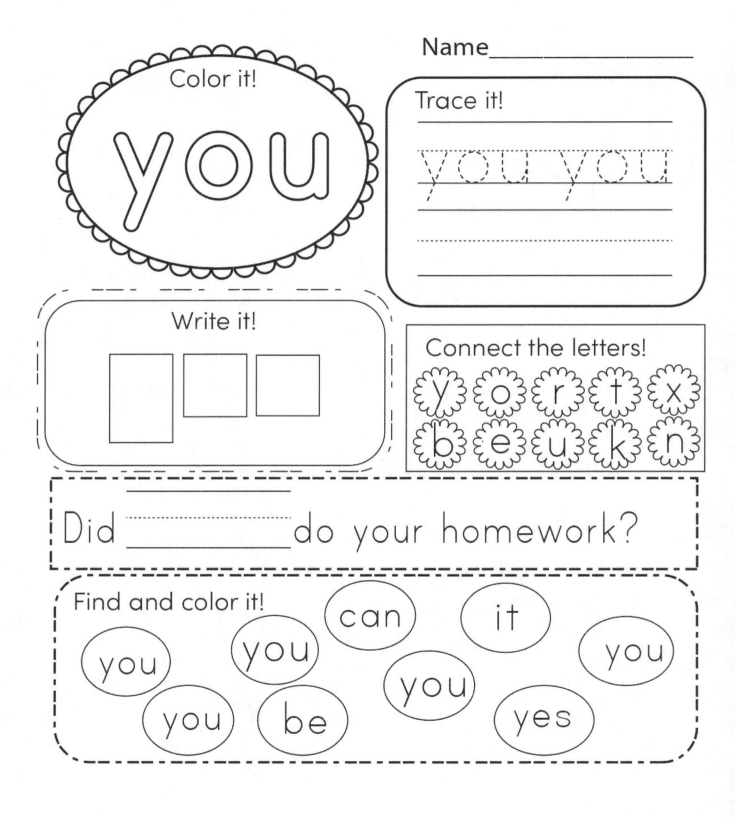

Name_____

**Color it!**

you

**Trace it!**

you you

**Write it!**

**Connect the letters!**

y o r t x
b e u k n

Did _____ do your homework?

**Find and color it!**

you    you    can    it    you
you    be    you    yes

# Sight Word - this

Name_____

### Color it!
this

### Trace it!
this

### Write it!

### Connect the letters!
t o i s v
p h m e x

Is _____ your book?

### Find and color it!
yes   play   this   this

this   can   this   this   come

# Sight Word – here

Name_____

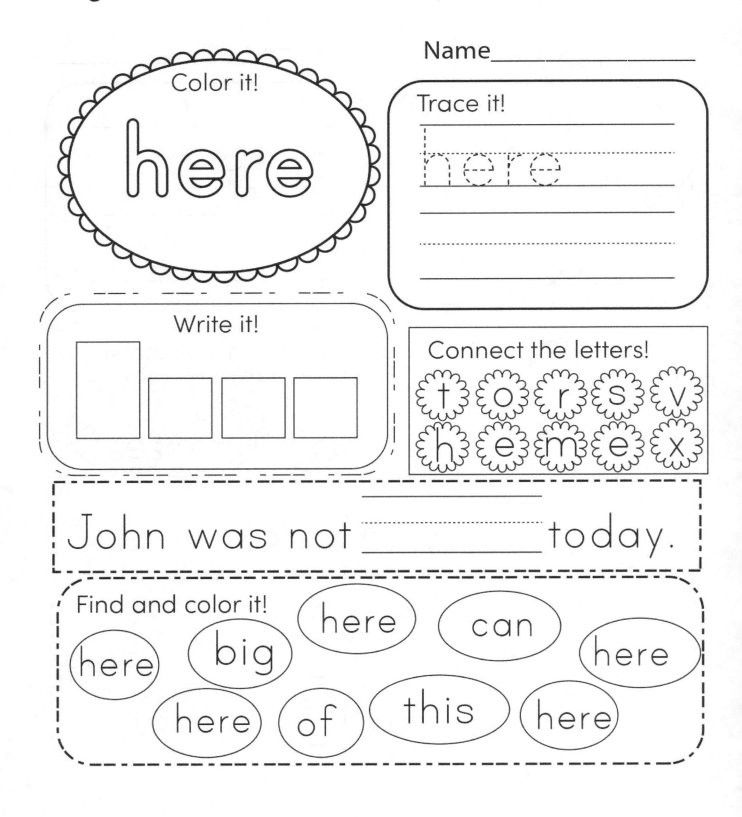

Color it!

here

Trace it!

here

Write it!

Connect the letters!

t  o  r  s  v
h  e  m  e  x

John was not _____ today.

Find and color it!

here   big   here   can   here

here   of   this   here

# Sight Word - she

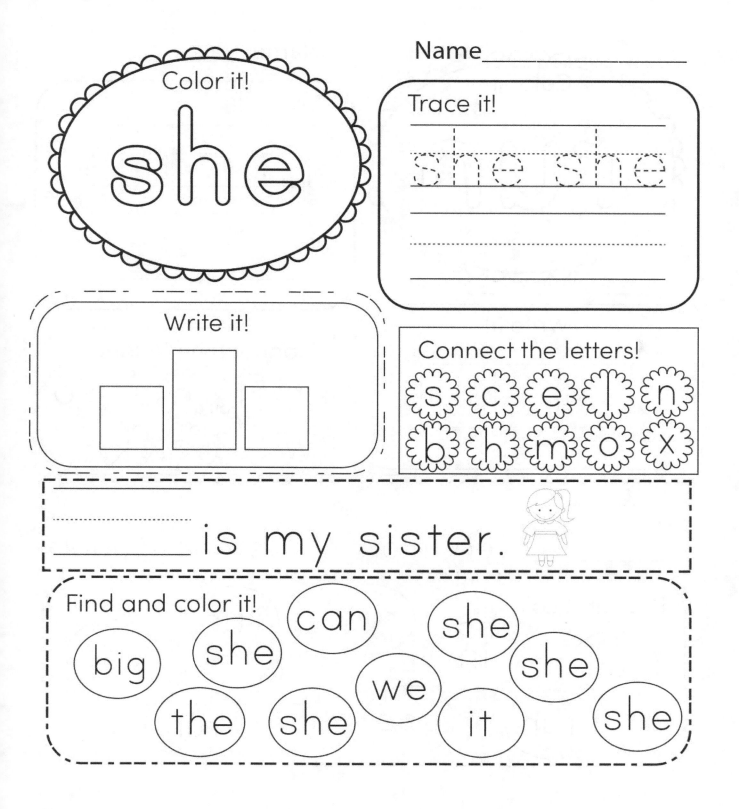

**Color it!**

she

Name_____

**Trace it!**

she she

**Write it!**

**Connect the letters!**

s c e l n
b h m o x

_____ is my sister.

**Find and color it!**

big she can she

she

the she we it she

# Sight Word - run

Name_____

Color it!

## run

Trace it!

run   run

Write it!

Connect the letters!

r t n z o
w u e k m

_____

I _____ every morning before school.

Find and color it!

run   in   run   run   one
run   see   to   run

# Sight Word - off

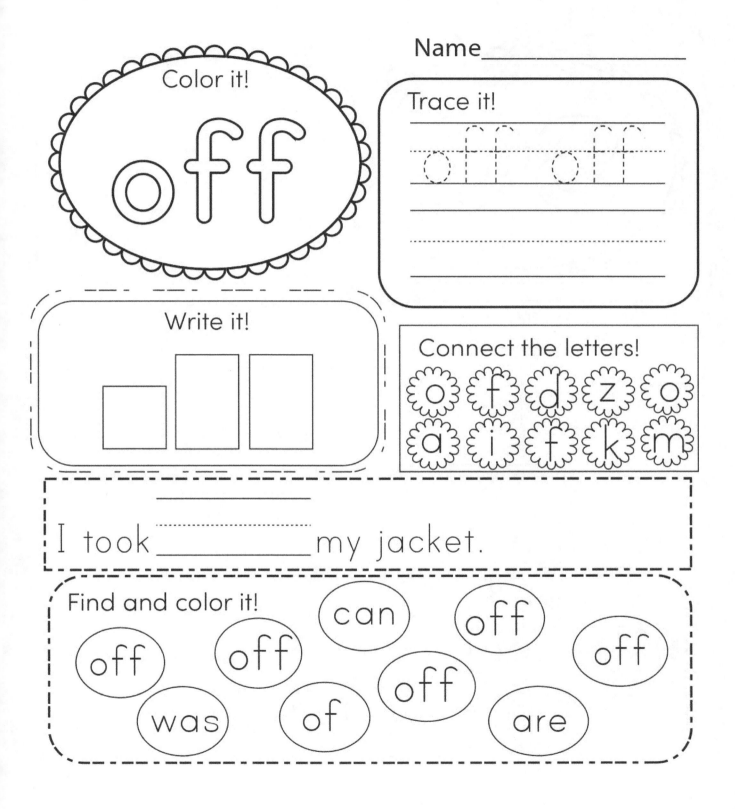

Color it!

off

Name_____

Trace it!

off    off

Write it!

Connect the letters!

o  f  d  z  o
a  i  f  k  m

I took_____my jacket.

Find and color it!

off    off    can    off

off

was    of    off    are

# Sight Word - so

Color it!

Name_____

Trace it!

Write it!

Connect the letters!

You are _____ nice!

Find and color it!

# Sight Word - want

Name_____

## Color it!
want

## Trace it!
want

## Write it!

## Connect the letters!
c  a  b  y  i
w  l  n  t  x

Do you _____ to go to the zoo?

## Find and color it!
yes   want   come   want   want
want   can   want   like

# Sight Word - do

Name_____

**Color it!**

do

**Trace it!**

do   do

**Write it!**

**Connect the letters!**

d  n  b  n  a

c  o  s  m  z

_____ you have any brothers?

**Find and color it!**

do   do   in   do

do   no   do   be   of   do

# Sight Word - and

Name_____

**Color it!**

and

**Trace it!**

and and

**Write it!**

☐ ☐ ☐

**Connect the letters!**

a  e  c  x  s
w  n  d  k  n

_____

I watched a movie with Beth_____Claire.

**Find and color it!**

and  in  and  eat  and

like  and  and  can

# Sight Word - what

Name_____

**Color it!**

what

**Trace it!**

what

**Write it!**

**Connect the letters!**

t   o   a   t   v
w   h   m   e   x

_____ is your name?

**Find and color it!**

yes   what   what   this   what

what   can   what   it

# Sight Word - little

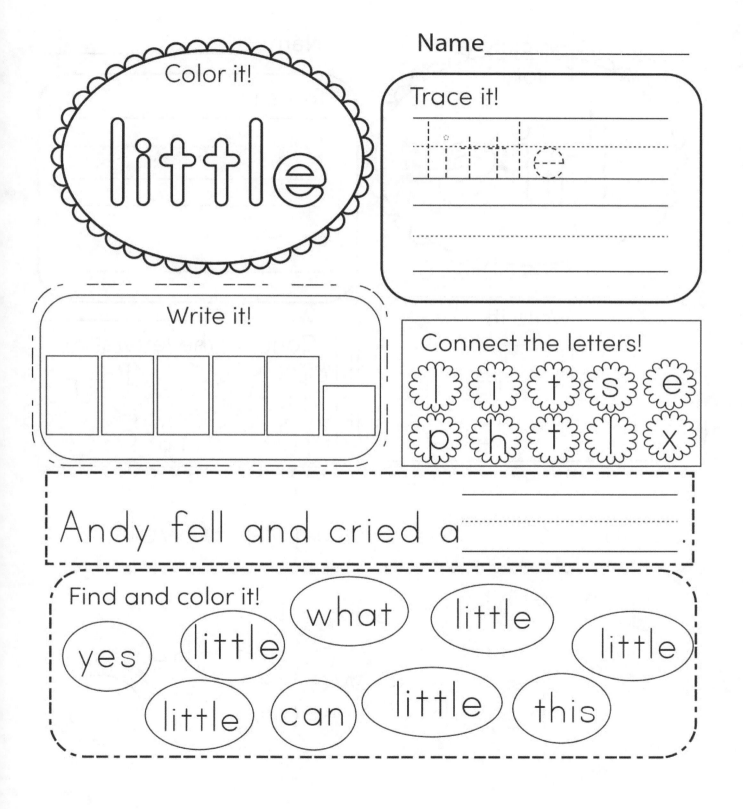

**Color it!**

little

Name_____

**Trace it!**

little

**Write it!**

**Connect the letters!**

l  i  t  s  e
p  h  t  l  x

Andy fell and cried a _____.

**Find and color it!**

yes    little    what    little    little
little    can    little    this

# Sight Word - his

Name_____

**Color it!**

his

**Trace it!**

his  his

**Write it!**

**Connect the letters!**

t  c  s  l  n
h  i  m  o  x

John took _____ dog on a walk.

**Find and color it!**

his  she  his  his  she
the  his  we  his  his

# Sight Word - two

Name_____

**Color it!**

t w o

**Trace it!**

two two

**Write it!**

**Connect the letters!**

v a o z o
t w s k m

I have _____ eyes.

**Find and color it!**

can    two
two    of        two
      off
was    two        two

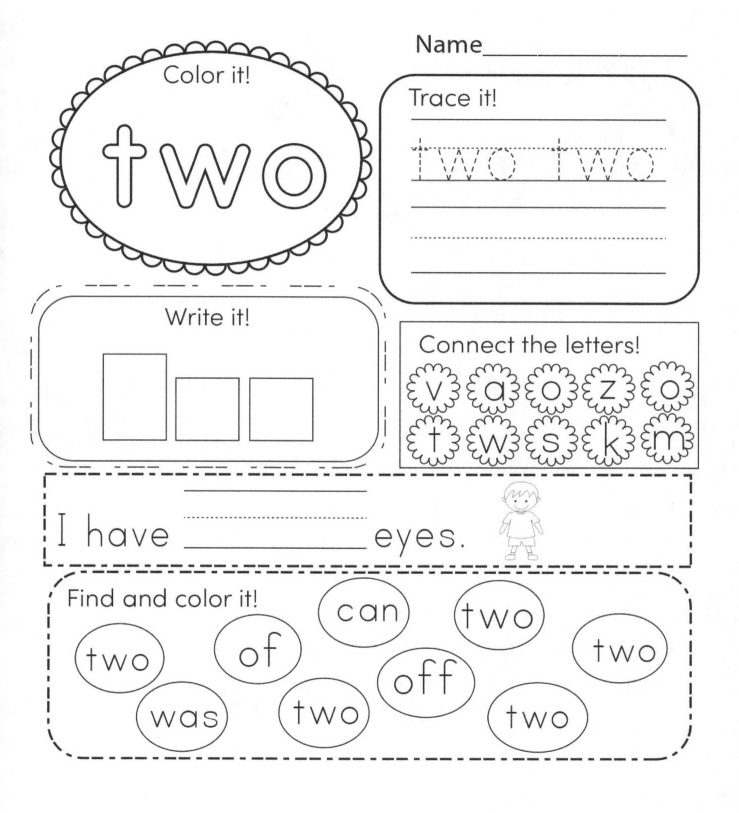

# Sight Word - love

Name_____

## Color it!

love

## Trace it!

love

## Write it!

## Connect the letters!

n o k e h
l i v t w

I _____ my pets.

## Find and color it!

love    be    love    yes    love
    love    can    like    love

# Sight Word - but

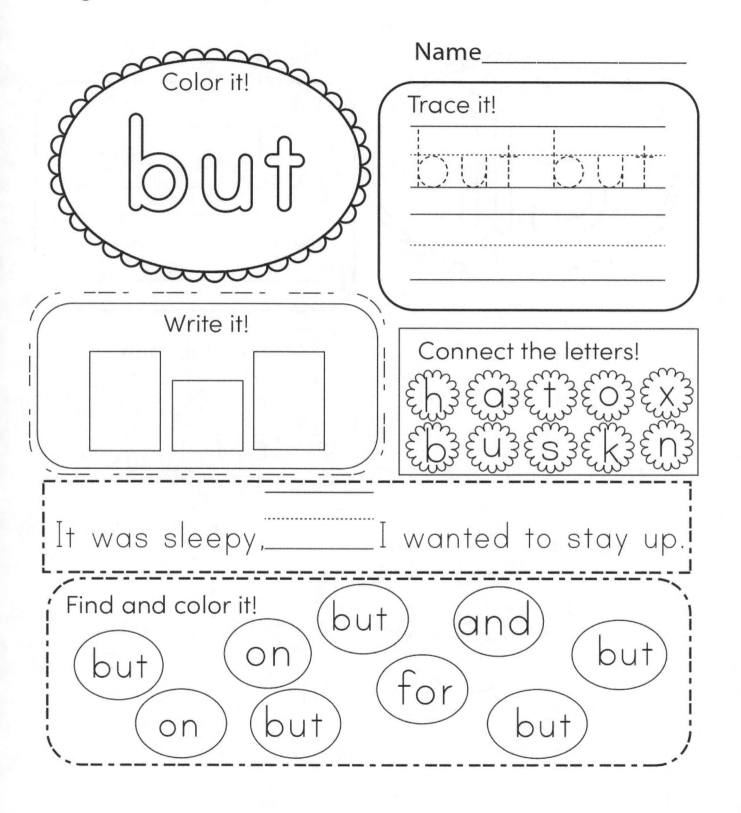

**Color it!**

but

Name_____

**Trace it!**

but but

**Write it!**

**Connect the letters!**

h a t o x
b u s k n

It was sleepy,_____ I wanted to stay up.

**Find and color it!**

but    on    but    and    but

on    but    for    but

# Sight Word - all

Name_____

## Color it!

all

## Trace it!

all   all

## Write it!

## Connect the letters!

a  e  c  x  s
w  l  l  k  n

John ate_____the cookies.

## Find and color it!

all   in   and   all   can
like   all   all   all

# Sight Word - saw

Name_____

## Color it!

saw

## Trace it!

saw

## Write it!

☐ ☐ ☐

## Connect the letters!

r a n z o
s u w k m

_____
I_____a bird flying across the sky.

## Find and color it!

saw   in   saw   saw   saw
she   saw   to   run

# Sight Word - said

Name_____

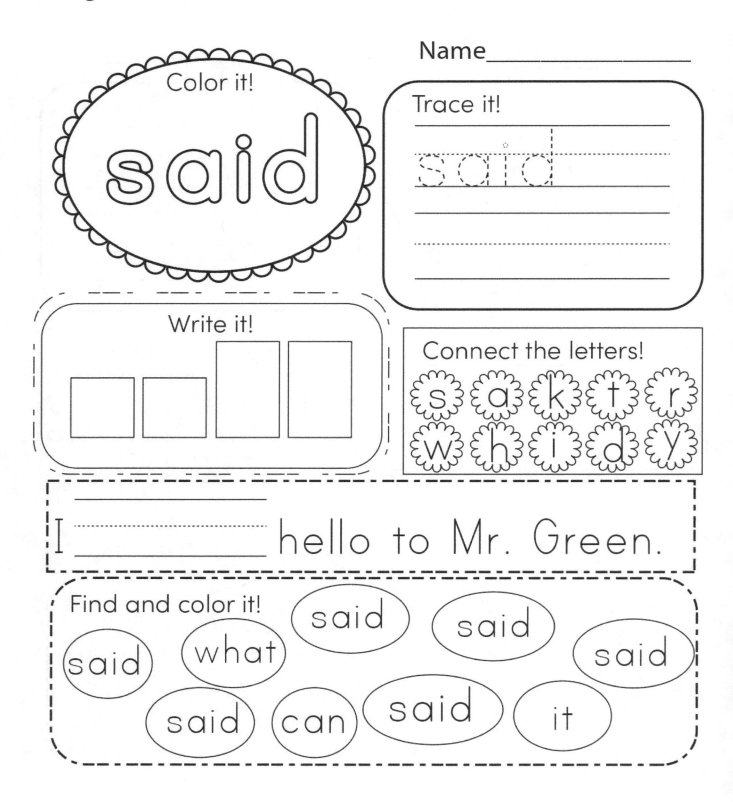

Color it!

said

Trace it!

said

Write it!

Connect the letters!

s a k t r
w h i d y

I _____ hello to Mr. Green.

Find and color it!

said    what    said    said    said

said    can    said    it

# Sight Word - there

Name_____

**Color it!**

there

**Trace it!**

there

**Write it!**

**Connect the letters!**

t o a r b
w h e e s

_____
Are _____ any frogs in this pond?

**Find and color it!**

what    there

yes    there    there

there    can    there    it

# Sight Word - him

**Color it!**

him

Name_____

**Trace it!**

him  him

**Write it!**

**Connect the letters!**

s c e l n
h i m o x

I asked _____ to sing.

**Find and color it!**

him  him  can  she
the  him  him  her  him  his

# Sight Word - that

Color it!

**that**

Name_____

Trace it!

that

Write it!

Connect the letters!

t o a t i
w h m e q

Is _____ your bag?

Find and color it!

yes  that  that  this  that
what  can  that  of

# Sight Word - got

Name_____

**Color it!**

got

**Trace it!**

got got

**Write it!**

☐ ☐ ☐

**Connect the letters!**

y o t r x
g e u k n

I _____ up at six o'clock.

**Find and color it!**

you    got    can    got
got    be    got    got    yes

# Sight Word - not

Name_____

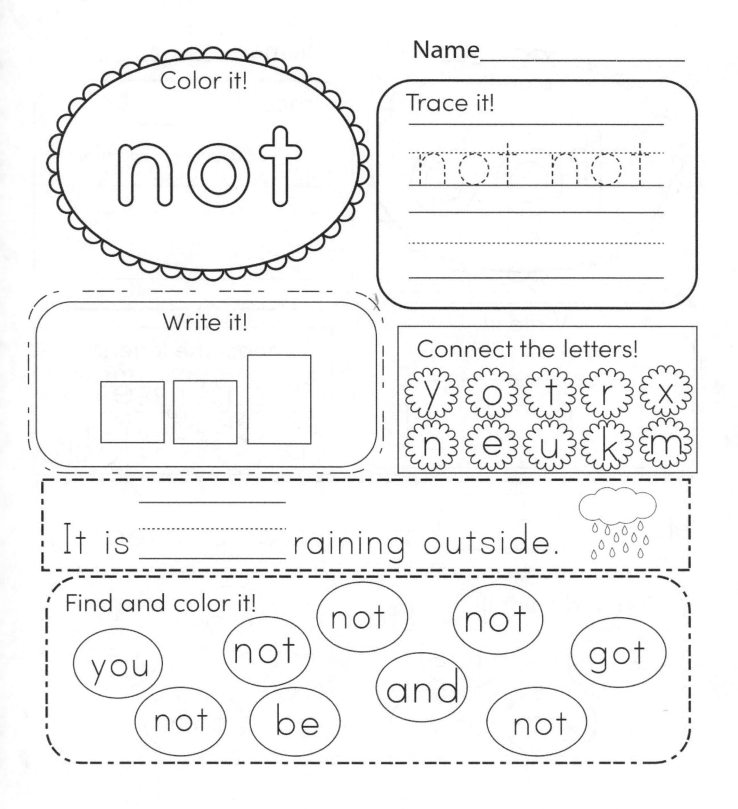

Color it!

**not**

Trace it!

not not

Write it!

Connect the letters!

y o t r x
n e u k m

It is _____ raining outside.

Find and color it!

you    not    not    not

not    be    and    not    got

# Sight Word - too

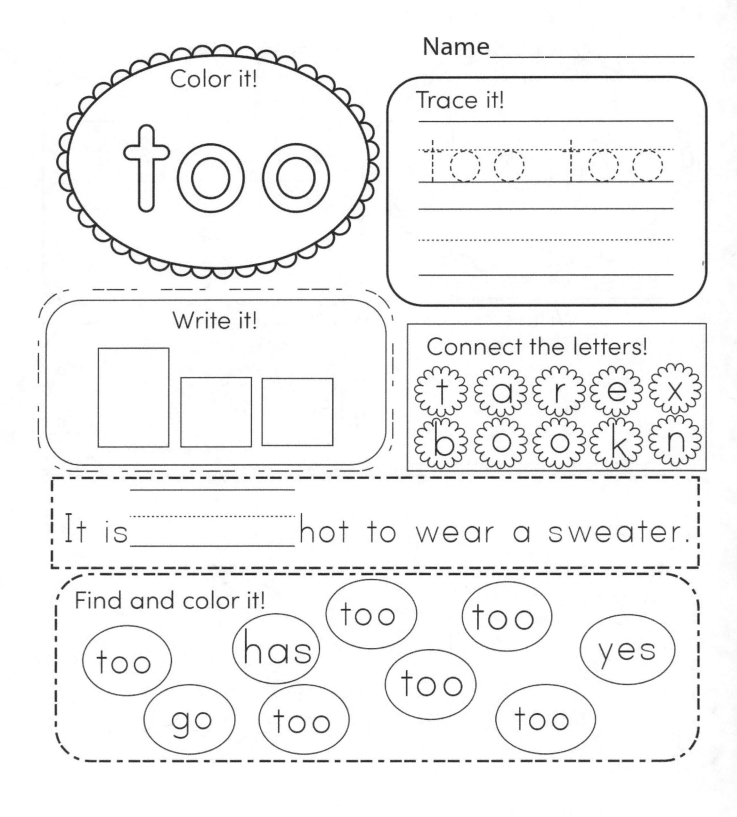

Color it!

Name_____

Trace it!

too too

Write it!

Connect the letters!

t a r e x
b o o k n

It is _____ hot to wear a sweater.

Find and color it!

too    has    too    too    yes
too    go    too    too    too

# Sight Word - why

**Name**_____

### Color it!
why

### Trace it!
why

### Write it!

### Connect the letters!
s c y l n
w h m o x

_____ did you fall?

### Find and color it!
why  why  can  why  was  the  she  why  it  why

# Sight Word - first

Name_____

### Color it!

first

### Trace it!

first

### Write it!

### Connect the letters!

f i r s e
p h a l t

My sister had her_____ birthday.

### Find and color it!

yes    first    first    first

little    can    first    this

# Sight Word - new

**Name**_____

**Color it!**

new

**Trace it!**

new

**Write it!**

☐ ☐ ☐

**Connect the letters!**

y  o  w  r  x

n  e  u  k  m

_____
I got a _____ backpack.

**Find and color it!**

you    new    new    not    new

new    be    and    new

# Sight Word - he

Name_____

**Color it!**

he

**Trace it!**

he   he

**Write it!**

**Connect the letters!**

a e r n k
h b b q p i

_____ is my brother.

**Find and color it!**

on
be   we      he
            he      he   a
   he   he      it

# Sight Word - as

Color it!

**as**

Name_____

Trace it!

as   as

Write it!

Connect the letters!

a  e  r  n  o
w  s  q  p  u

I am_____tall_____John.

Find and color it!

on   as   as
be   we   as
as   is   as   it

# Sight Word - look

Name_____

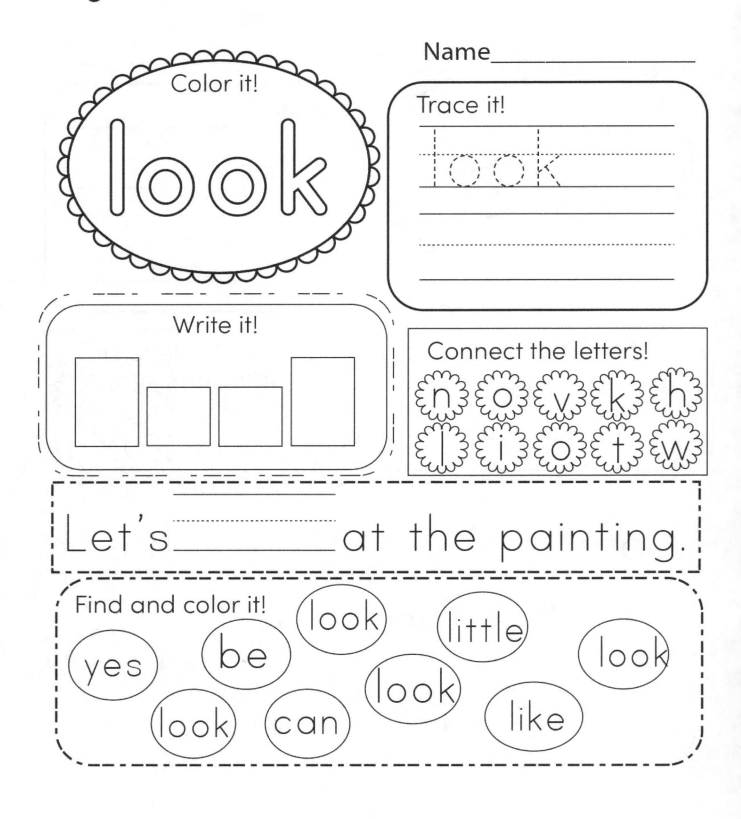

Color it!

## look

Trace it!

look

Write it!

Connect the letters!

n o v k h
l i o t w

Let's _____ at the painting.

Find and color it!

look    little    look
yes    be    look
look    can    like

# Sight Word - with

Name_____

### Color it!
with

### Trace it!
with

### Write it!

### Connect the letters!
s i k h r
w h t d e

I went to the zoo_____ Amy.

### Find and color it!
said   with   was   with   with
with   can   with   it

# Sight Word - they

Name_____

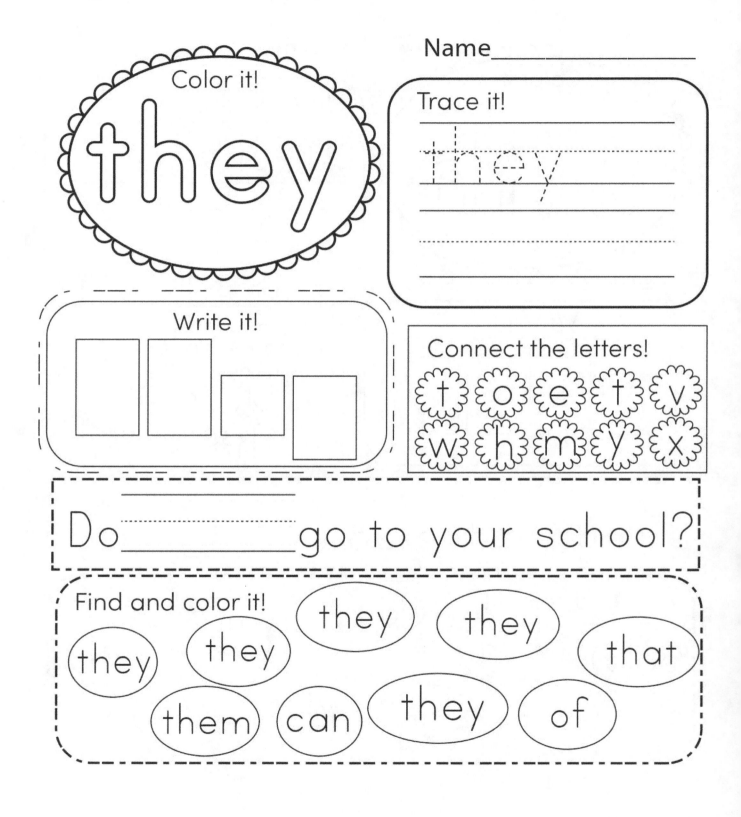

**Color it!**
they

**Trace it!**
they

**Write it!**

**Connect the letters!**
t o e t v
w h m y x

Do_____go to your school?

**Find and color it!**
they    they    they    that
they    them    can    they    of

# Sight Word - three

## Color it!

three

Name_____

## Trace it!

three

## Write it!

## Connect the letters!

t    i    r    e    e

p    h    t    l    x

_____

I have _____ sisters.

## Find and color it!

yes   three   three   three   three

three   can   three   this

# Sight Word - six

Name_____

**Color it!**

six

**Trace it!**

six   six

**Write it!**

**Connect the letters!**

S   i   o   z   o
t   w   x   k   m

I turned _____ years old yesterday.

**Find and color it!**

six   six   can   six
was   six   off   six   six

# Sight Word - where

**Color it!**

where

Name_____

**Trace it!**

where

**Write it!**

**Connect the letters!**

t o a r b
w h e s e

_____
_____ do you live?

**Find and color it!**

yes    where    where    where    there

where    can    where    that

# Sight Word - day

Name_____

**Color it!**

day

**Trace it!**

day

**Write it!**

**Connect the letters!**

d a m l n
w h y o x

It is a sunny _____ .

**Find and color it!**

why  day  can  day  was
day  she  day  big  day

# Sight Word - could

Name_____

### Color it!
could

### Trace it!
could

### Write it!

### Connect the letters!
t o u r b
c h e l d

I _____ see the stars last night.

### Find and color it!
yes    there    could    could
could    can    could    got    could

# Sight Word - my

Name_____

**Color it!**

my

**Trace it!**

my  my

**Write it!**

**Connect the letters!**

m a i c z
e y k s r

I went to the park with _____ friend.

**Find and color it!**

he · in · my · my · me
my · my · my · by · up

# Sight Word - me

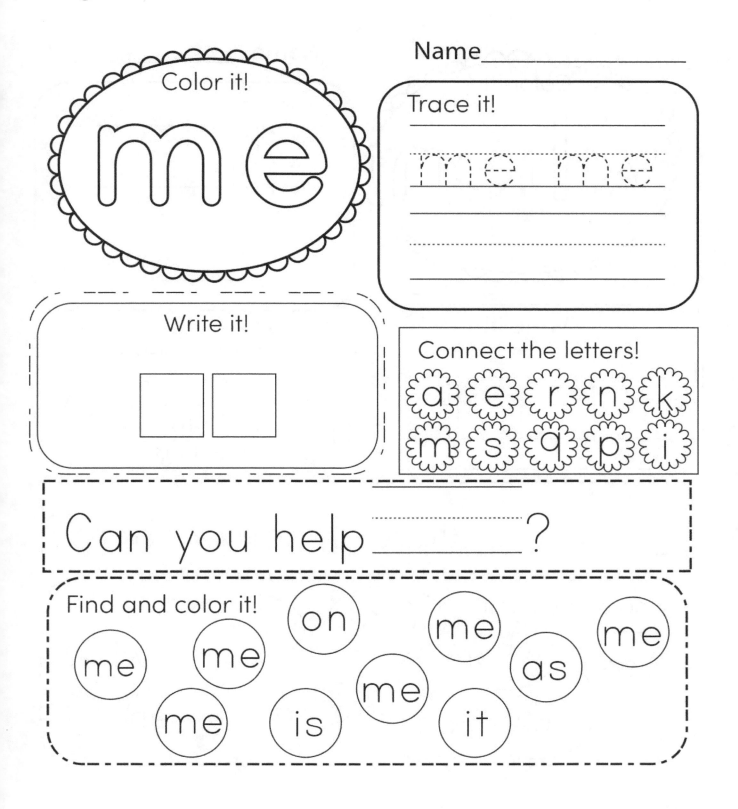

**Color it!**

m e

Name_____

**Trace it!**

me  me

**Write it!**

☐ ☐

**Connect the letters!**

a  e  r  n  k

m  s  q  p  i

Can you help_____?

**Find and color it!**

me   me   on   me   me

me   is   me   it   as

# Sight Word - when

Name_____

**Color it!**

when

**Trace it!**

when

**Write it!**

**Connect the letters!**

t o e n v
w h m a x

_____ did you come home?

**Find and color it!**

yes  when  what  this  when

when  can  when  when

# Sight Word - jump

**Color it!**

jump

Name_____

**Trace it!**

jump

**Write it!**

**Connect the letters!**

j u e p v
w h m y x

John can _____ really high.

**Find and color it!**

jump  jump  jump  that
jump
them  can  jump  of

# Sight Word - went

Name_____

## Color it!

went

## Trace it!

went

## Write it!

☐ ☐ ☐ ☐

## Connect the letters!

c  e  b  y  i
w  l  n  t  x

I _____ to Megan's birthday party.

## Find and color it!

yes   went   went   went   went
want   with   went   like

# Sight Word - four

Name_____

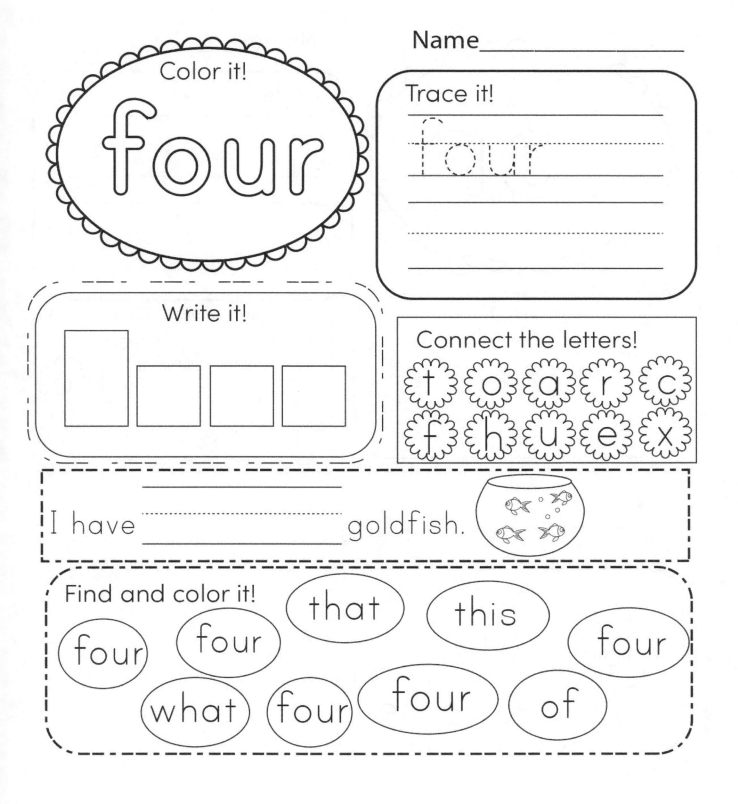

Color it!

**four**

Trace it!

four

Write it!

Connect the letters!

t o a r c
f h u e x

I have _____ goldfish.

Find and color it!

four · four · that · this · four
what · four · four · of

# Sight Word - ten

Name_____

**Color it!**

ten

**Trace it!**

ten ten

**Write it!**

**Connect the letters!**

s  i  n  z  o
t  e  x  k  m

I went to Mike's house at_____o'clock.

**Find and color it!**

ten    ten
ten    to          ten
was         the    ten    six

# Sight Word - get

**Color it!**

get

Name_____

**Trace it!**

get   get

**Write it!**

**Connect the letters!**

g  u  t  p  c
w  e  m  y  n

Where did you _____ this?

**Find and color it!**

get   get   go   get   get

them   get   jump   get

# Sight Word - away

Name_____

**Color it!**

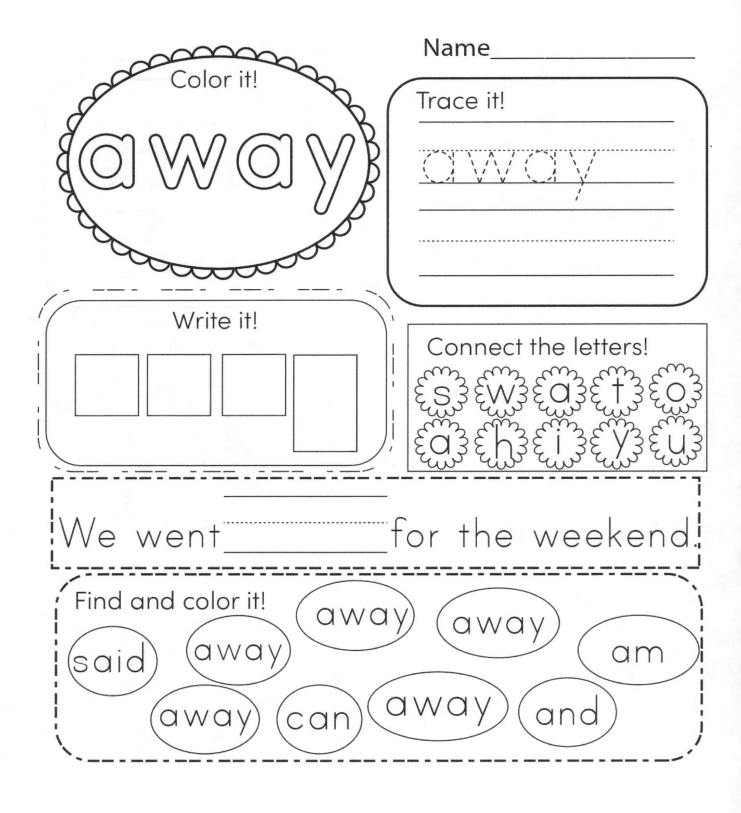

away

**Trace it!**

away

**Write it!**

**Connect the letters!**

s w a t o

a h i y u

We went_____for the weekend.

**Find and color it!**

said   away   away   away   am

away   can   away   and

# Sight Word - came

Color it!

**came**

Name_____

Trace it!

came

Write it!

Connect the letters!

c a d y i
p l m e u

Pat _____ from Georgia.

Find and color it!

do   came   came   came   came
am   can   come   came

# Sight Word - five

Name_____

**Color it!**

five

**Trace it!**

five

**Write it!**

**Connect the letters!**

t  i  a  t  i
f  h  v  e  g

I had dinner at_____ o'clock.

**Find and color it!**

five    that    five    five    five    five    can    five    of

# Sight Word - seven

Name_____

**Color it!**

seven

**Trace it!**

seven

**Write it!**

**Connect the letters!**

s e u n b
c v e l d

I got up at_____o'clock.

**Find and color it!**

seven    seven

yes    there    seven

seven    can    seven    got

# Sight Word - eight

Name_____

### Color it!
eight

### Trace it!
eight

### Write it!

### Connect the letters!
s i g n t
e v a h d

An octopus has _____ legs.

### Find and color it!
ten   eight   eight   eight   eight
seven   can   eight   eight

# Sight Word - your

Name_____

**Color it!**

your

**Trace it!**

your

**Write it!**

**Connect the letters!**

y o a r c
f h u e x

Where is_____ house?

**Find and color it!**

your    four    your    your    your

what    you    your    of

# Sight Word - because

Name_____

### Color it!

**because**

### Trace it!

because

### Write it!

### Connect the letters!

b a u s b
e c i l e

I ran home_____it started to rain.

### Find and color it!

yes   because   because   could   because

because   can   because   got

# Sight Word - out

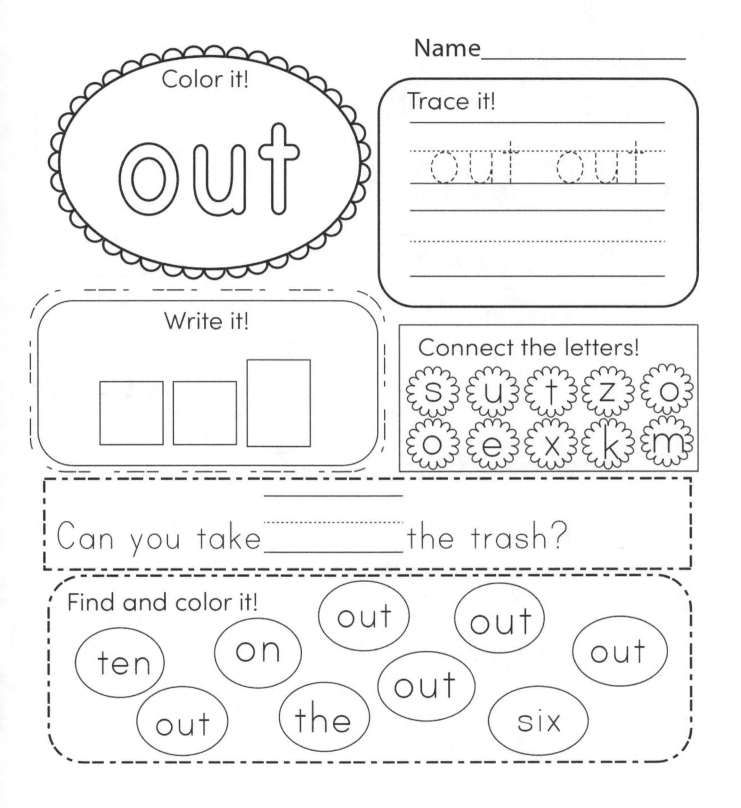

**Color it!**

out

Name_____

**Trace it!**

out   out

**Write it!**

**Connect the letters!**

s u t z o
o e x k m

Can you take_____the trash?

**Find and color it!**

ten   on   out   out   out
out   the   out   six

# Sight Word - from

Name_____

Color it!

from

Trace it!

from

Write it!

Connect the letters!

n r v k h
f i o m w

Paul is _____ Canada.

Find and color it!

from    be    from    for    from

from    can    look    from

# Sight Word - who

Name_____

**Color it!**

who

**Trace it!**

who who

**Write it!**

**Connect the letters!**

W h x z o
t a o k m

_____ did you talk to yesterday?

**Find and color it!**

with  who  who  who  we
was  six  who  who

# Sight Word - her

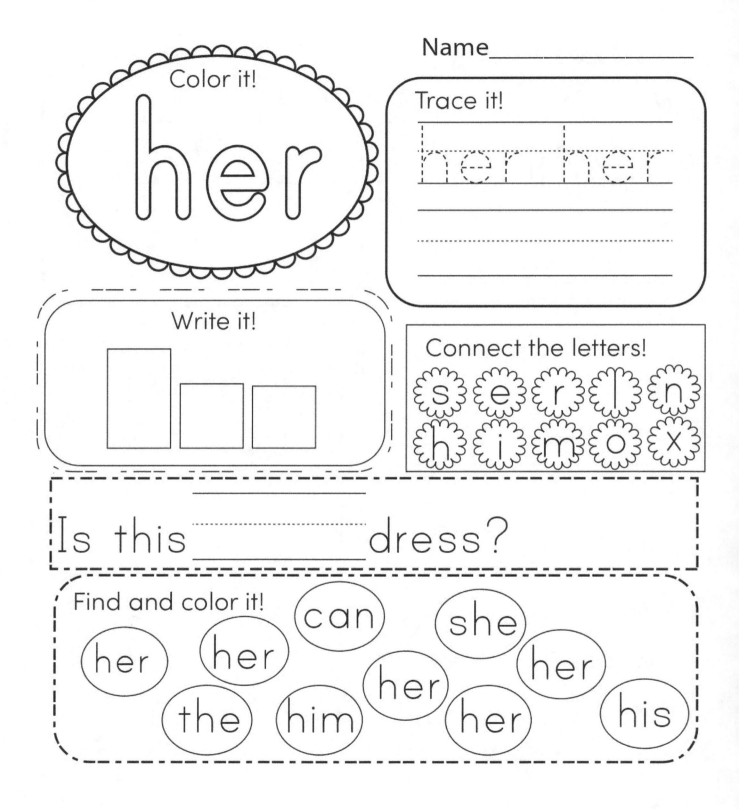

**Color it!**

her

Name_____

**Trace it!**

her her

**Write it!**

**Connect the letters!**

s e r l n
h i m o x

Is this _____ dress?

**Find and color it!**

her   her   can   she

the   him   her   her   her

his

# Sight Word - then

Name_____

**Color it!**

then

**Trace it!**

then

**Write it!**

**Connect the letters!**

t  o  e  t  i
w  h  m  n  q

_____
I ate breakfast and _____ went to school.

**Find and color it!**

yes    then    then    that    then

this    can    then    to

# Sight Word - yellow

Name_____

**Color it!**

yellow

**Trace it!**

yellow

**Write it!**

**Connect the letters!**

b  e  l  s  o
y  c  i  l  w

I saw a _____ butterfly.

**Find and color it!**

yes   yellow   yellow   yellow   yellow

yellow   can   yellow   got

# Sight Word - red

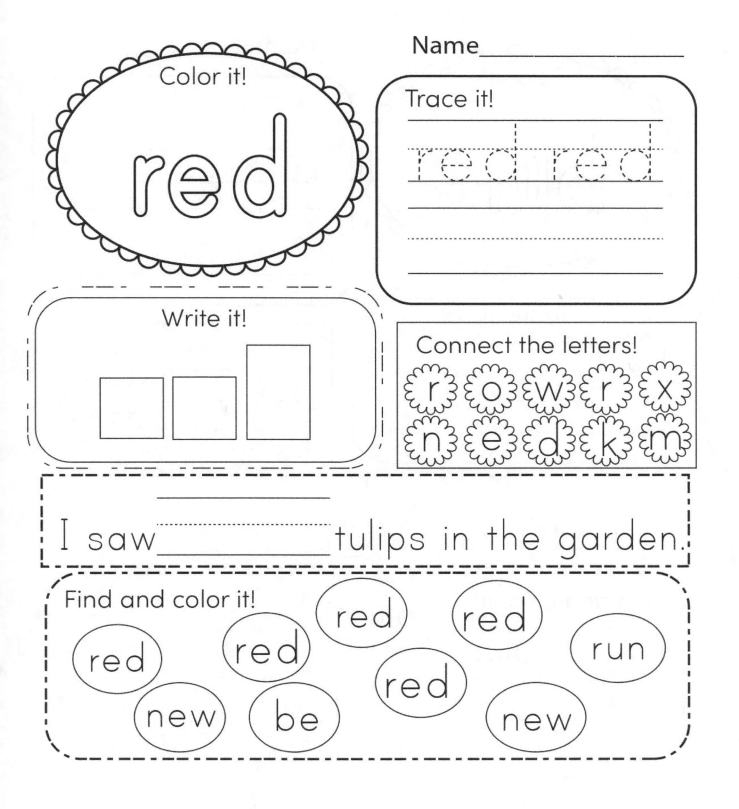

**Color it!**

red

**Name**_____

**Trace it!**

red red

**Write it!**

**Connect the letters!**

r o w r x
n e d k m

I saw _____ tulips in the garden.

**Find and color it!**

red   red   red
new   be   red   run
      red   new

# Sight Word - blue

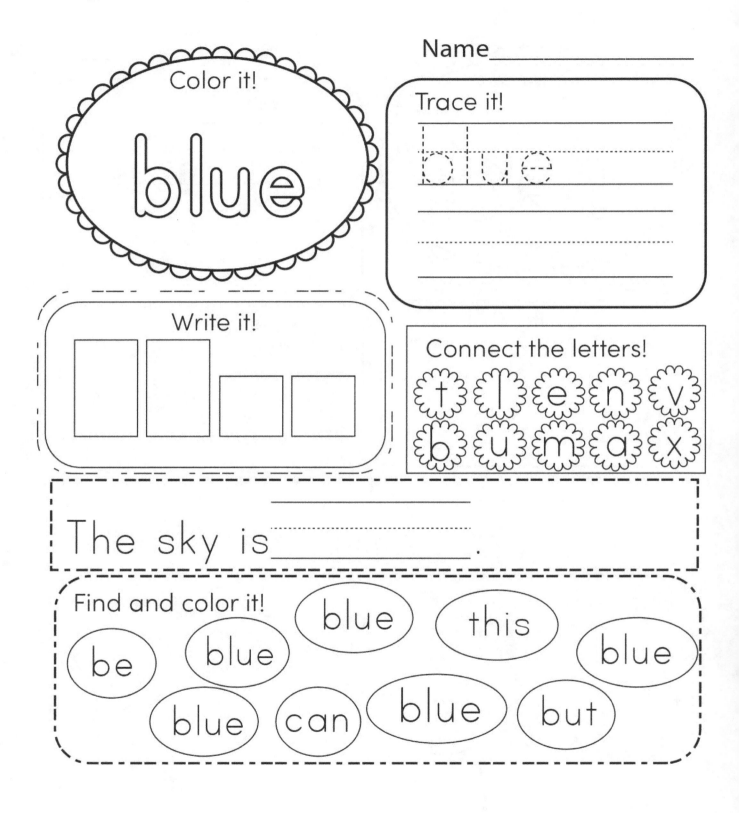

Color it!

blue

Name_____

Trace it!

blue

Write it!

Connect the letters!

t l e n v
b u m a x

The sky is_____.

Find and color it!

blue    this

be    blue    blue

blue    can    blue    but

# Sight Word - white

Name_____

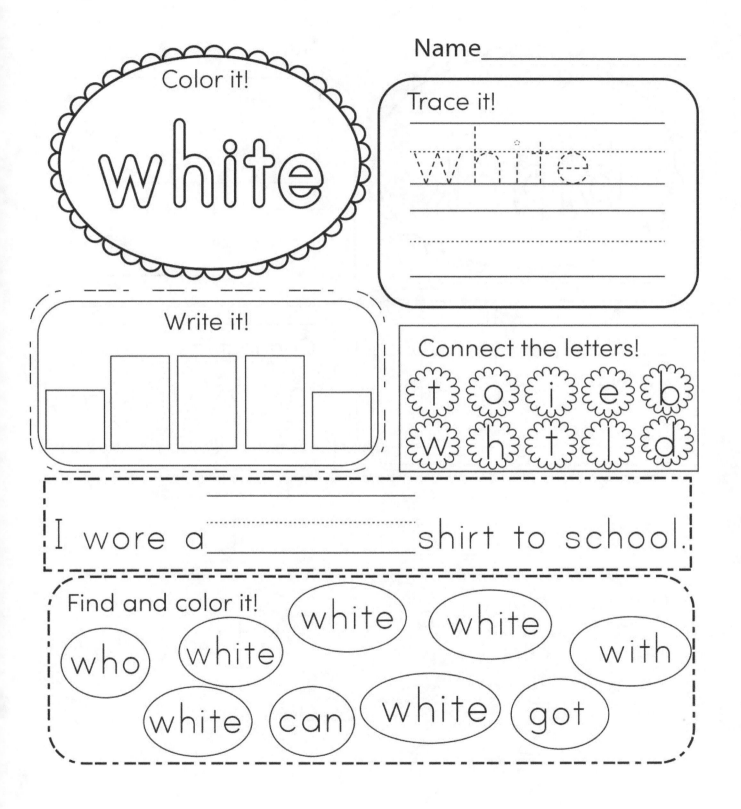

**Color it!**

white

**Trace it!**

white

**Write it!**

**Connect the letters!**

t  o  i  e  b
w  h  t  l  d

I wore a _____ shirt to school.

**Find and color it!**

who   white   white   white   with
white   can   white   got

# Sight Word – black

Name_____

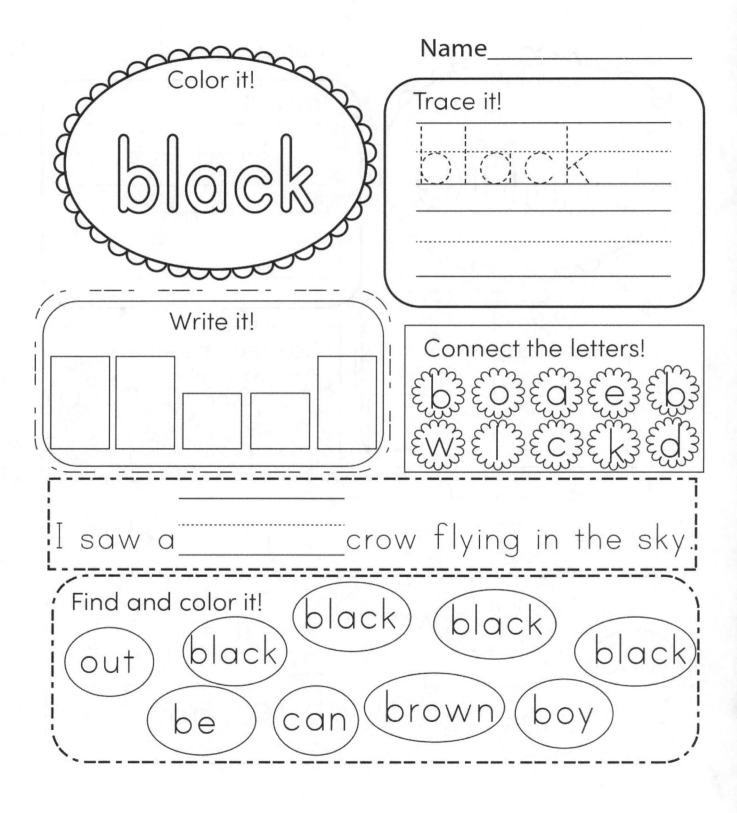

**Color it!**
black

**Trace it!**
black

**Write it!**

**Connect the letters!**
b  o  a  e  b
w  l  c  k  d

I saw a _____ crow flying in the sky.

**Find and color it!**
out   black   black   black   black
be   can   brown   boy

# Sight Word - brown

Color it!

brown

Name_____

Trace it!

brown

Write it!

Connect the letters!

b o w e b
r l c n d

I have _____ eyes.

Find and color it!

be  brown  brown  brown  black

brown  can  brown  boy

# Sight Word - green

Name_____

### Color it!
green

### Trace it!
green

### Write it!

### Connect the letters!
b r e e a
g l c x n

The grass is _____ .

### Find and color it!
get    green    green    green
green
brown    got    green    go

# Sight Word - purple

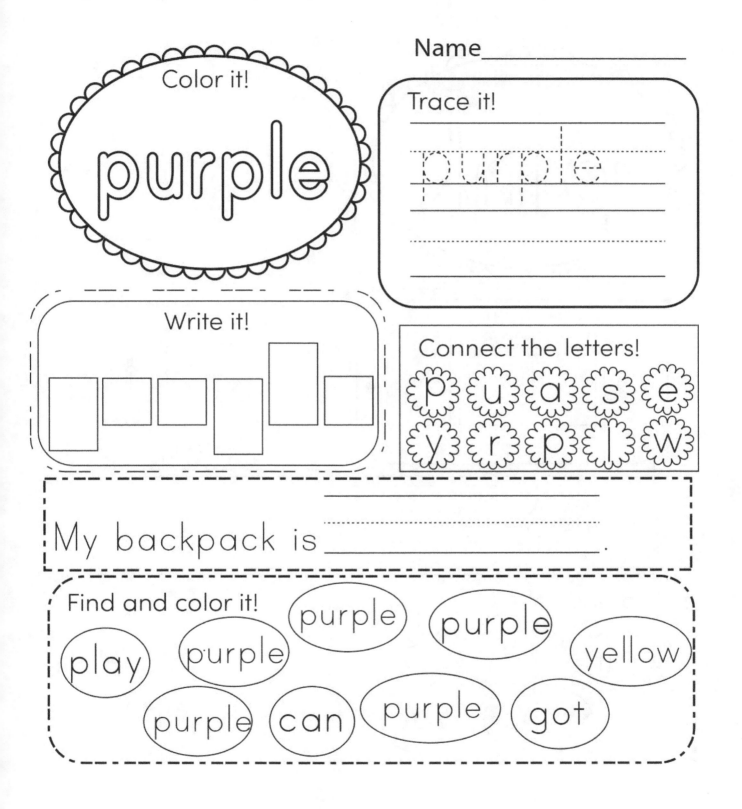

**Color it!**

purple

Name_____

**Trace it!**

purple

**Write it!**

**Connect the letters!**

p u a s e
y r p l w

My backpack is _____.

**Find and color it!**

play  purple  purple  purple  yellow

purple  can  purple  got

# Sight Word - pink

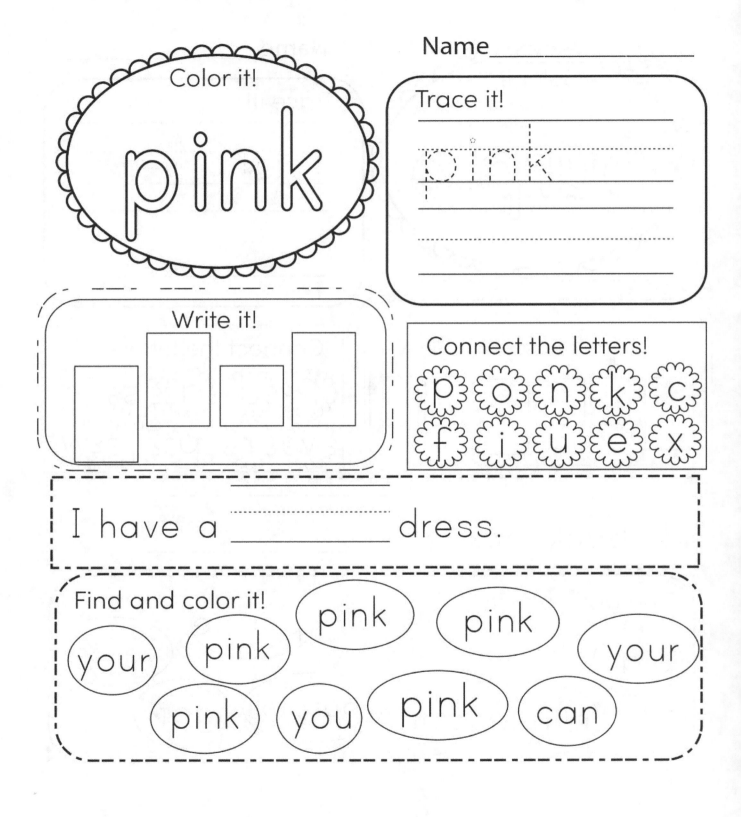

Name_____

**Color it!**

pink

**Trace it!**

pink

**Write it!**

**Connect the letters!**

p  o  n  k  c
f  i  u  e  x

I have a _____ dress.

**Find and color it!**

your  pink  pink  pink  your
pink  you  pink  can

# Sight Word - nine

**Name**_____

## Color it!

nine

## Trace it!

nine

## Write it!

## Connect the letters!

n e b e i
w i n t x

_____

I picked_____apples.

## Find and color it!

new    nine

yes    nine    not

nine    with    nine    like

# Sight Words Flash Cards

I

can

we

the

at

am

# Sight Words Flash Cards

Name_____

it

up

no

yes

like

a

# Sight Words Flash Cards

Name_____

see

go

in

of

us

by

# Sight Words Flash Cards

Name_____

eat

was

to

have

is

play

# Sight Words Flash Cards

Name_____

come

on

be

big

one

has

# Sight Words Flash Cards

Name_____

are

for

you

this

here

she

# Sight Words Flash Cards

Name_____

run

off

so

want

do

and

# Sight Words Flash Cards

Name_____

what

little

his

two

love

but

# Sight Words Flash Cards

Name_____

all

saw

said

there

him

that

# Sight Words Flash Cards

Name_____

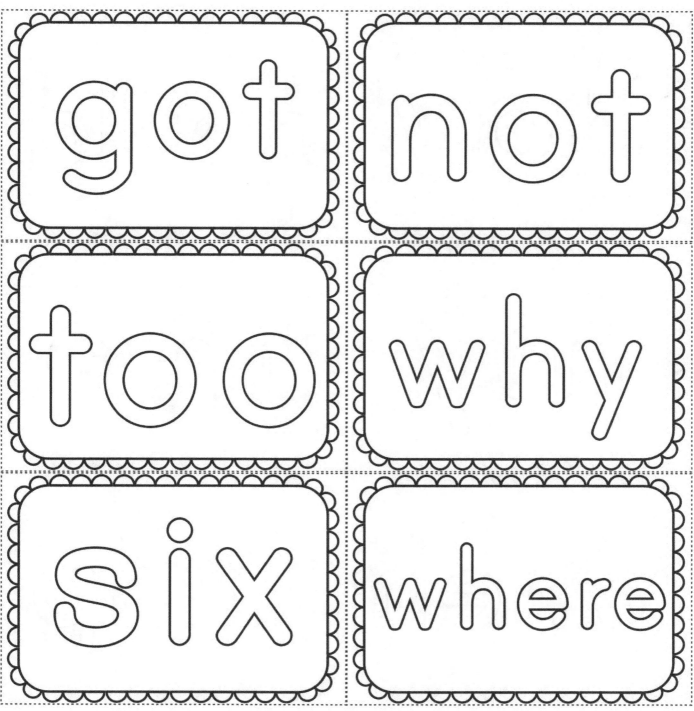

# Sight Words Flash Cards

Name_____

day

could

my

me

when

jump

# Sight Words Flash Cards

Name_____

went

first

new

he

as

look

# Sight Words Flash Cards

Name_____

with

they

three

your

because

out

# Sight Words Flash Cards

Name_____

from

who

her

then

yellow

red

# Sight Words Flash Cards

four

ten

get

away

came

five

# Sight Words Flash Cards

Name_____

Name_____

seven

eight

blue

white

black

brown

# Sight Words Flash Cards

Name_____

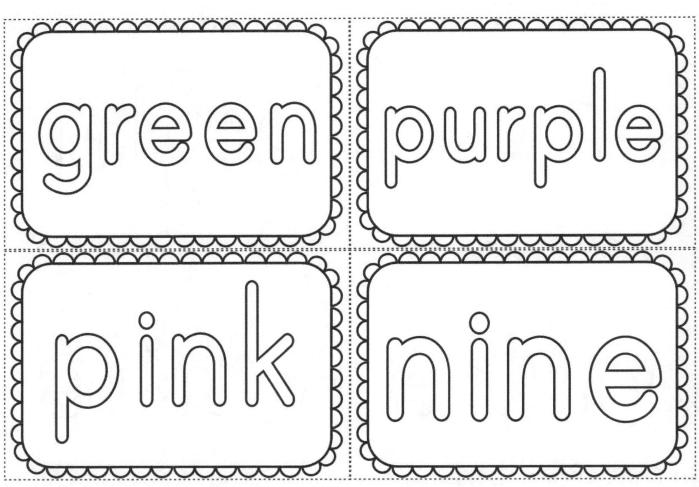

green

purple

pink

nine

# More From Author

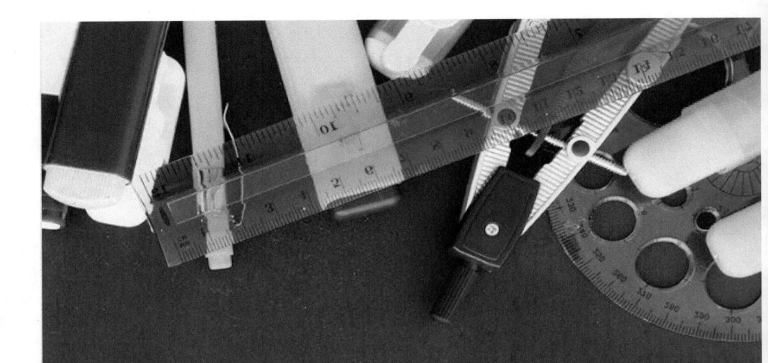

THANK
YOU